Lie Low

Ciara Elizabeth Smyth

T0191063

methuen | drama

LONDON • NEW YORK • OXFORD • NEW DELHI • SYDNEY

METHUEN DRAMA
Bloomsbury Publishing Plc
50 Bedford Square, London, WC1B 3DP, UK
1385 Broadway, New York, NY 10018, USA
29 Earlsfort Terrace, Dublin 2, Ireland

BLOOMSBURY, METHUEN DRAMA and the Methuen
Drama logo are trademarks of Bloomsbury Publishing Plc

First published in Great Britain 2022

A catalogue record for this book is available from the British Library.

A catalog record for this book is available from the Library of Congress.

ISBN: PB: 978-1-3505-1727-1
ePDF: 978-1-3505-1729-5
eBook: 978-1-3505-1728-8

Series: Modern Plays

Typeset by Mark Heslington Ltd, Scarborough, North Yorkshire

To find out more about our authors and books visit
www.bloomsbury.com and sign up for our newsletters.

CAST

Faye	Charlotte McCurry
Naoise/Duck Man	Thomas Finnegan
Doctors VO	Rory Nolan

CREATIVE TEAM

Director	Oisín Kearney
Set and Lighting Designer	Ciaran Bagnall
Sound Designer	Denis Clohessy
Movement Director	Paula O'Reilly
Fight Coordinator	Philip Rafferty
Stage Manager	Ciara Nolan

Ciara Elizabeth Smyth | Playwright

Ciara Elizabeth Smyth is an award-winning playwright from Dublin. Her plays have been presented by the Abbey Theatre, the Project Arts Centre, Bewley's Cafe Theatre, Dublin Fringe Festival, the Lyric Theatre, Belfast, and the Traverse Theatre, Edinburgh. She is currently under commission with several television production companies and theatre companies across the UK and Ireland. Her play *Lie Low* won Best Theatre Script award at the Writers Guild of Ireland Awards 2023 and was also awarded First Finalist BBC Writers Room Popcorn Award 2023, as well as being nominated for Best New Play and Best Actress at the Irish Times Theatre Awards 2022. *Lie Low* will tour the UK in 2024, starting with a run in The Royal Court. Ciara's debut short film, *SLAY + PREPARE*, will premiere in 2024 and she is also on commission to develop a debut feature film. Ciara is represented by Curtis Brown.

Charlotte McCurry | Cast – Faye

Charlotte is an award-winning actress from Belfast. She trained at Guildford School of Acting and was the recipient of the Sir Alec Guinness Memorial Award.

Previous work includes: *Lie Low* (Dublin Fringe Festival & Edinburgh Fringe), *The Twilight Zone* (Almeida West End), *Oedipus*, *She Stoops to Conquer*, *The Risen People*, *The Dead*, *The Picture of Dorian Gray* (Abbey Theatre), *The Father*, *The Threepenny Opera* (Gate Theatre Dublin), *Big Maggie*, *DruidShakespeare*, *Conversations on a Homecoming* (Druid), *Northern Star* (Rough Magic), *Double Cross*, *Alice The Musical*, *Beauty and the Beast*, *Little Red*, *The Jungle Book*, *The Crucible* (Lyric Theatre Belfast), *Annie* (Cork Opera House), *Nivelli's War* (Lyric Theatre/ New Victory Theatre New York/ Cahoots NI), *Pinocchio* (The Mac/ Cahoots NI), *Hedda* (Green Room), *Both Sides* (Ransom), *The Great Carmo!* (Cahoots NI), *The Haunting of Helena Blunden* (Big Telly), *The Famous Five*

(Tabard Theatre), *Kitty* and *Damnation* (Lion & Unicorn), *Jack & the Beanstalk* (Grand Opera House Belfast).

Television work includes: *Ellis* (Channel5/ Company Pictures), *Say Nothing* (FX/ Minim Productions), *Silverpoint* (BBC), *World on Fire* (BBC), *Dalgliesh* (Channel5/Acorn TV), *Hope Street* (BBC), *Ted's Top Ten* (CITV), *Almost Never* (CBBC), *Three Families* (BBC), *The Titanic Inquiry* and *Our William* (BBCNI). Film work includes: *Ballywalter* (Empire Street Productions).

For her portrayal of Faye in *Lie Low*, Charlotte won Best Performer at Dublin Fringe Festival Awards 2022 and was nominated for Best Actress in the Irish Times Theatre Awards 2023.

Thomas Finnegan | Cast – Naoise

Thomas is from Newry, Co Down. He took part in the Lyric Drama Studio and appeared in their production of *Our Country's Good*. He went on to train at the Royal Welsh College of Music and Drama, appearing in *VS09* and *You Can't Take It With You*.

Since graduating he has performed across all mediums. TV credits include: *Game of Thrones*, *Line of Duty*, *Ups and Downs*, *The Windermere Children*, and season two of *Blue Lights*. Radio credits include: *The Fewness of His Words*, *Locked in*, and *Not Now*.

Onstage he has appeared in the Lyric Theatre productions *Blackout*, *Here Comes the Night*, *Lovers: Winners and Losers* and *Romeo and Juliet*, Ciara Elizabeth Smyth/Prime Cut Productions' previous production of *Lie Low* at the Abbey Theatre Dublin/Traverse Theatre Edinburgh, and the Lyric Theatre/Prime Cut co-production of *Red*, for which he was nominated for an Irish Times Award for Best Supporting Actor.

Oisín Kearney | Director

Oisín is a writer and director who works across stage, screen and radio. He is represented by Curtis Brown and worked as assistant director on Belfast Lyric Theatre productions during 2016–20. Directing credits: *Lie Low* (Dublin Fringe Festival), *New Speak* (Lyric Theatre), *I Banquo* and *My Left Nut*. Oisín has directed several documentaries for BBC Northern Ireland and De Correspondent/NPO2. His first feature as director, *Bojayá: Caught in the Crossfire*, premiered at Hot Docs Film Festival in Toronto in April 2019, and he has assistant-produced feature documentaries, including *66 Days* (BBC Storyville) and Oscar long-listed and Emmy-nominated *Elián* (CNN Films). He was co-writer of *My Left Nut* ('Show in a Bag' and BBC Three series, winner of Best Drama in the Royal Television Society Northern Ireland Awards), *The Alternative* (winner of two Irish Times Theatre Awards and nominated for Best New Play) and *The Border Game* (opened in Belfast International Arts Festival 2021 and toured Ireland).

Ciarán Bagnall | Set & Lighting Designer

Ciarán is the Creative Director for Prime Cut Productions. He trained at the Royal Welsh College of Music & Drama in Cardiff and was made a fellow of the College in 2017.

In 2022 he was the Assistant Artistic Director of the Opening Ceremony of the Commonwealth Games in Birmingham.

In 2023 he was made an Honorary Member of the Chinese Institute of Stage Design and was presented a special award for international communication.

His work was used to represent Irish Theatre Design at the Prague Quadrennial International Exhibition (PQ) in 2019 and he was invited back to exhibit again in 2023.

Recent set & lighting designs include: *Animal Farm* (UK Tour), *The Beauty Queen of Leenane* (Prime Cut/Lyric Theatre,

Belfast – Winner Best Play Revival UK Theatre Awards), *Of Mice and Men* (Birmingham Rep/UK Tour), *Hangmen* (Gaiety Theatre, Dublin), *Cavalcaders* (Druid Theatre Company/ Irish Tour), *X'ntigone* (Prime Cut/MAC/Abbey Theatre, Dublin), *Rough Girls*, *A Streetcar Named Desire*, *RED*, *Lovers* (Lyric, Belfast), *The Whip* (RSC), *A Christmas Carol*, *The Great Gatsby* (Gate, Dublin), *The Merchant of Venice* (Great Theatre, Shanghai), *UBU The King*, *The Man Who Fell to Pieces*, *Hard to be Soft*, *Lally the Scut*, *The God of Carnage*, *Villa*, *Discurso*, *Tejas Verdes* (MAC, Belfast), *The Train*, *Observe the Sons of Ulster Marching Towards the Somme* (UK Tour/Abbey Theatre, Dublin); *Macbeth* (Shakespeare's Globe, London); *Othello* (RSC).

www.ciaranbagnalldesign.com

Denis Clohessy | Sound Designer

Denis has been producing work with Junk Ensemble for more than 10 years. He has also worked with The Abbey Theatre, The Gate Theatre, CoisCéim, Rough Magic, Fishamble, Corn Exchange, Northlight Theatre, Chicago and Beijing Children's Art Theatre. He won the Irish Times Theatre Award for Best Soundscape in 2011 and 2019. He was also a nominee in 2015 for Junk Ensemble and Brokentalker's *It Folds*. Denis was an associate artist with the Abbey in 2008 and was a participant on Rough Magic's ADVANCE programme in 2012.

Composition for film and television includes the feature films *One Night In Millstreet* (Fastnet Films), *The Confessors* (Atom Films), *Older than Ireland* (Snackbox Films), *His and Hers* (Venom Film), *The Irish Pub* (Atom Films), *The Land of the Enlightened* (Savage Film), *In View* (Underground Cinema), *The Reluctant Revolutionary* (Underground Films), the television series *The Limits of Liberty* (South Wind Blows) performed by the RTE Concert Orchestra and the Will Sliney (Marvel Comics) animation series *Storytellers* (Fastnet Films).

Paula O'Reilly | Movement Director

Theatre credits: *Little Women* (The Lyric, Belfast), *Hansel &
Gretel* (The Lyric, Belfast), *Rapunzel – A Tangled Pantomime*
(GBL Productions at The Waterfront Hall, Belfast), *Some
Where Out There You* (The Abbey Theatre, Dublin), *The Beauty
Queen of Leenane* (Primecut Productions & The Lyric,
Belfast), *Lie Low* (Ciara Elizabeth Smyth, Primecut
Productions, The Abbey Theatre Dublin & The Traverse),
The Half Moon (The Lyric, Belfast & The Pleasance Dome),
The Beauty Queen of Leenane (Primecut Productions & The
Lyric Belfast), *Tartuffe* (The Abbey Theatre, Dublin &
National Tour), *Silent Trade* (Kabosh, The Lyric Belfast & NI
Tour), *Aladdin* (GBL, The Waterfront, Belfast), *Bridesmaids of
Northern Ireland* (GBL, The Grand Opera House Belfast),
Callings (Kabosh), *Distortion* (The MAC), *The Shedding of Skin*
(Kabosh), *Secrets of Space* (Cahoots NI, The MAC Belfast &
USA Tour), *The Snapper*, *Revival* (The Gate Theatre, Dublin),
The Odd Couple (The Everyman, Cork), *Bigger People* (The
Local Group and Pentabus), *In Our Veins* (Bitter Like A
Lemon and The Abbey Theatre), *The Tales of Hoffmann* (Irish
National Opera), *The Snapper* (The Gate), *Harder, Faster, More*
(Red Bear Productions at The Project), *Acis & Galetea*
(Ireland National Opera at The National Opera House and
National Tour), *Herculaneum* (Wexford Festival Opera),
Cristina Regina di Svezia, *Le Roi Malgre Lui*, *A Village Romeo &
Juliet*, *The Magic Flute* (Wexford Festival Opera), *Orfeo ed
Euridice* (Buxton Opera Series).

Philip Rafferty | Fight Coordinator

Philip is a stage combat instructor and fight director based in
Belfast. He is a member of the Academy of Performance
Combat & Raff Combat, and has taught in Rose Bruford
College, Lyric Theatre Belfast and Belfast Metropolitan
College. Fight directing credits: *The Beauty Queen of Leanne*
(Prime Cut, Lyric Theatre), *Lie Low* (Abbey Theatre, Lyric
Theatre), *Good Vibrations* (Lyric Theatre, Island Arts Centre),

Tosca (Grand Opera House, Belfast), *Vection* (Lyric Theatre, Belfast) and *Little Women* (Lyric Theatre, Belfast).

Ciara Nolan | Stage Manager

Ciara has been a freelance stage manager for many years and is a graduate of The Lir Academy. Some of Ciara's theatre credits are: Caoimhe O'Malley's *Prickly*, Jennifer Laverty's *Standing in Lifts With Strangers*, Ciara Elizabeth Smyth's *Lie Low* and *Sauce*, Jack Thorne's *Mydidae*, Brendan Behan's *Borstal Boy*, Disney's *Beauty and the Beast*, *Wicked*, *My Fair Lady*, *Shrek the Musical* and Gaiety Pantos.

Prime Cut Productions

**Prime Cut Productions
Unit 5, 8 Maxwell St
Belfast, BT12 5FB**

Website: https://www.primecutproductions.co.uk
Facebook: https://www.facebook.com/PrimeCutProductions/
Twitter/X: https://twitter.com/prime_cut?lang=en
Instagram: https://www.instagram.com/
primecutproductions/

Established in 1992, Prime Cut Productions is an
Independent Theatre Producing Organisation based in
Belfast and is one of Northern Ireland's critically acclaimed
arts organisations. Excellence is at the core of our practice,
and we are committed to producing artistically engaging
experiences for our audiences and artists. Prime Cut has
produced over 60 highly acclaimed Northern Irish and Irish
Premieres of the best of International Theatre showcasing
the work of Northern Irish Theatre Artists across the island
of Ireland and beyond. The company currently produces
two to three full-scale productions per year, at least one of
which tours throughout the island of Ireland, UK and
internationally complemented by a programme of ancillary
activities.

Prime Cut delivers under three main strands: CREATE,
INNOVATE and PARTICIPATE.

- CREATE: Producing excellent performance and writing
  from Northern Ireland for an international audience.

- INNOVATE: Driving the development of Northern Irish Performing Artists by providing the finest professionals training, mentorships and opportunities.

- PARTICIPATE: Providing a creative resource promoting autonomy and artistic self-expression for communities across Northern Ireland with trust and collaboration at its heart.

Since 2013 our CREATE productions and co-productions have received 20 awards across the UK, Ireland, Europe and Australia. Prime Cut Productions have also been the recipients of the BBC Performing Arts Fellowship, three Weston Jerwood Creative Bursaries, Allianz Arts & Business Board Member of the Year Award (2015) and our Artistic Director Emma Jordan was awarded the Breakthrough Fund in Cultural Entrepreneurship by the Paul Hamlyn Foundation and the 2015 Spirit of Festival Award at the Belfast International Arts Festival.

Acknowledgements

Thank you to:

Mum and Dad for your constant support and love.

Gavin Kostick and everyone at Fishamble: The New Play Company.

Ruth McGowan, Bee Sparks and all at Dublin Fringe Festival.

Lucy Ryan at Smock Alley Theatre.

Alex Cusack and Peter Reid at Reboot Festival.

Caoimhe Connolly and Cliona Dukes at Scene+Heard – A Festival of New Work. Thank you for everything. I am far from the only person who owes their beginning to you.

All at the Irish Theatre Institute, thank you for giving me a home.

All our supporters and associates: The MAC Theatre Belfast, Prime Cut Productions, The Mill Theatre Dundrum, An Táin Arts Centre, Paul Meade, Dun Laoghaire-Rathdown County Council and The Arts Council Ireland.

Cian O'Brien and all at Project Arts Centre, Dublin.

Jimmy Fay and all at the Lyric Theatre, Belfast.

Sonya Kelly for responding to me while you were in the midst of opening your own play.

Pamela McQueen, Eleanor White, Roddy Doyle and Conor McPherson for taking the time to read the play and for your words of encouragement.

Aoibheann McCann and Roseanna Purcell for all your work during the development stage.

Our gorgeous creative team. I'm so lucky to have had you working on this.

Enda Walsh, for your enthusiasm, wild generosity and genius.

I still can't believe you answer my emails.

My wonderful agents Katie Battcock, Nick Marston and all at Curtis Brown, I'm grateful every day for you.

Mark O'Rowe, for the hours you spent reading and discussing this play with me.

Your kindness, encouragement and brilliance are, in no small part, the reason the script was finished at all.

Thomas and Charlotte, you make the play infinitely better. Thank you for saying yes.

Mick, I wrote this play for you. It wouldn't exist without. Thank you for changing my life.

And finally, thank you Oisín, for everything.

Lie Low
(or Paranotica)

For Michael

Characters

Faye Carver, *thirties/forties, female*
Naoise Carver, *thirties/forties, male*
Dr Houlihan/Dr Hollowman, *forties/fifties, male*
Duck Man, *male*

Notes

Set somewhere in Ireland.

If adapting for your geographical location, feel free to change words which do not work in your idiom and context; i.e. 'Aye' could be replaced with Yeah/Ouais/ايوا, etc.

Minimum on-stage cast is two actors.

Doctors *can be recorded as voiceover (V/O) – at the director's discretion.*

Punctuation is used to indicate delivery, not to conform to the rules of grammar.

/ denotes an interruption by another character speaking.

– denotes an interruption by action or thought or difficulty continuing the sentence.

. . . denotes a character trailing off.

Content warning: the text contains strong language, and references to depression, nudity and sexual violence.

Refrain One

Swing

A woman stands on stage.
She's wearing red lipstick, red nail polish and a long skirt.
Her hair looks blow dried.
This is **Faye**.
Behind her, a light flashes, illuminating a wardrobe.
A throbbing light comes from inside it that draws **Faye**'s *attention.*
The wardrobe door opens slowly and a person wearing a yellow duck
mask steps out. This is **Duck Man**.
Faye *and* **Duck Man** *stand staring at each other for a moment.*
Suddenly, a drum beat starts and something seriously swingy comes
on.
Something like Sing, Sing, Sing by Benny Goodman.
Faye *and* **Duck Man** *break into a swing dance.*
Faye *is really enjoying it.*
As **Faye** *twirls,* **Duck Man** *pulls a pair of red, silk knickers out of*
her pocket.
Duck Man *sniffs the knickers deeply.*
Faye *starts to miss steps.*
Duck Man *spins her in, squeezes her, then dips her.*
It looks like they might kiss for a moment.
They don't.
Duck Man *spins* **Faye** *into the spotlight and leaves.*
Music snaps off.

One

The Last Doctor Said No

A doctor's surgery, somewhere in Ireland.

Faye   I was having nightmares.

Dr Houlihan   Okay.

Faye   That's how it started off, I kept having these nightmares.

Dr Houlihan   And what would happen in the nightmares?

Faye   The usual stuff. Sometimes I'd be falling.

Dr Houlihan   Classic.

Faye   Or I'd lose my voice.

Dr Houlihan   Typical.

Faye   Or an enormous penis would chase me through a meadow full of yellow rubber ducks and try to insert itself into my mouth.

Dr Houlihan   All fairly standard but dream interpretation is not really my area.

Faye   No, I know.

Dr Houlihan   You know my father, who was also a GP, didn't even believe in dreams.

Faye   What?

Dr Houlihan   He didn't even believe in dreams. He was a challenging man.

Faye   Right.

Dr Houlihan   Anyway.

Faye   Anyway. It started with the nightmares. I'd wake up and I wouldn't be able to get back to sleep. Then I stopped being able to go to sleep. And now I can't sleep at all. I haven't slept in almost two weeks. Another doctor gave me sleeping tablets but they didn't really work.

Dr Houlihan   What do you worry about?

Faye   I don't know. Nightmares. Not sleeping. Someone hiding in the wardrobe.
Normal things.

Dr Houlihan   Has anything else been bothering you?

Faye   I think it's something physical. The insomnia. I'm a bit worried my mouth is too small.

Dr Houlihan   "Let's see."

Faye *opens wide and he shines a light around her mouth.*

Dr Houlihan   Looks fine.

Faye   Is there enough room for air and stuff?

Dr Houlihan   Plenty. It's quite a large cavity actually. Do you piss a lot?

Faye   Piss?

Dr Houlihan   Piss yeah, I like to be informal. How many times would you go? In the night, say.

Faye   Oh several. I'd say several.

Dr Houlihan   Right, and do you ever feel like you're better than everyone else?

Faye   In what context?

Dr Houlihan   I mean, are you ever talking to someone and you just think, 'I'd rather be talking to a vat of steaming hot bin juice than listening to one more word from this utter waste of kidneys'?

Faye   Sometimes.

Dr Houlihan   You know I think you might be bipolar.

Faye   Why?

Dr Houlihan   Female patients with urinary incontinence experience a variety of comorbid psychiatric disorders.

Faye   But I'm not incontinent.

Dr Houlihan   You are a bit. And if you are bipolar, you could be having a manic episode right now.

Faye   I don't think I am bipolar. I don't feel manic.

Dr Houlihan   Right. (*Cheerfully.*) Maybe you're depressed?

Faye   I don't feel depressed.

Dr Houlihan   Depression's sneaky like that though. Creeps in. Next thing you know you're using your finger to eat expired caviar in a public toilet. What about ADD? Do you feel ADD?

Faye   No.

Dr Houlihan   Oh! Autism!

Faye   No.

Dr Houlihan   There must be something wrong with you. How's your work?

Faye   I quit. I used to be a copywriter for a vegan meat company. But after a while I started to think what's the fucking point, you know? Eat the pig. Eat a fucking goat for all I care. So I didn't go back after my sick leave.

Dr Houlihan   Why were you on sick leave?

Faye   I was broken into a year ago and I was struggling for a bit afterwards. I'm fine now though.

Dr Houlihan   What happened?

Faye   Someone broke into my house and I walked in on them.

Dr Houlihan   What did they do?

Faye   Nothing really. He hit me. I passed out. When I woke up I had no knickers on and he was standing over me with his penis out.

Dr Houlihan   He took your knickers off?

Faye   I might have done that. I was stocious. I'd been at a party that night, taken off some of my clothes. As a joke, like, as part of a dance.

Dr Houlihan   Did you see this man's face?

Faye   No. I just saw his penis.

Dr Houlihan   Right. Wow. Heavy stuff. Sounds traumatic. Bit like a book. Do you think that's the reason you're not sleeping?

Faye   Well, it was a year ago. And I'm fine now. So no, I don't think it's related.

Dr Houlihan   Have you got someone to support you? A partner?

Faye   No, I'm single.

Dr Houlihan   What about parents?

Faye   My mother is dead. Cancer. My father's not well. Dementia, he's in a nursing home.

Dr Houlihan   Siblings?

Faye   A brother. But we're not close.

Dr Houlihan   Well, you need someone. Everyone needs someone.

Faye   I need to sleep. I just need to sleep. Look, you're the third doctor I've spoken to about this. I've tried medication, water, exercise, meditation, reading, routine, bathing, lavender, vitamins, minerals, no screens, more screens, white noise, sage, praying, counting sheep, hugging sheep, valium, hypnosis, I've literally tried everything.
So can you or can you not help me?

Two

So I Asked My Brother for Help

The wardrobe acts as a Mary Poppins bag for the set.
Items placed around the room:
A stool.
A large rock.
A mop.
A two-litre bottle of Diet Coke.
A box of Rice Krispies.
When everything is in its place, **Faye** *starts munching on dry Rice*
Krispies straight out of the box and **Naoise** *steps in.*
Naoise *is neatly dressed, wearing a scarf and holding a candle.*
They stand staring at each other, until . . .

Naoise   Your hair is lovely.

Faye   Do you like it?

Naoise   I do. It's dark.

Faye   It is dark.

Naoise   It's different but it really suits you.

Faye   Thank you. Felt like I needed a change, you know?
The blonde was a bit 'look at me'.

Naoise   Aye, well, it looks great.

Faye *eats a handful of Rice Krispies, then takes a long swig of Diet*
Coke.

Naoise   Sorry, have I interrupted your . . . dinner?

Faye   No, no.

Naoise   Will I leave you to finish?

Faye   Nat a'tall. This is just a snack. I'm trying to eat more.

Naoise   Aye. You've lost a good bit of weight. If you don't
mind me saying.

Faye   No I don't mind. I haven't been hungry is all.

Naoise   Sorry, Faye, I shouldn't have said that. Making a comment on your appearance. It's out of order.

Faye   It's alright, Naoise, I don't mind.

Naoise *looks around.*

Naoise   Did you move in recently?

Faye   No. Been here about eight months. Nine, maybe.

Naoise   Amazing. You have it very (*Beat.*) Scandinavian.

Faye   That's exactly what I was going for. You know I have almost no possessions now. It's very freeing.

Naoise (*nods*)   Mmmm. I just bought a new couch, would you like my old couch?

Faye   I don't want a couch.

Faye *puts down the Krispies and takes another swig of Diet Coke.*

Faye   How's Hazel?

Naoise   She's fine. She's good. I brought you this.

He hands her the candle.

Faye   Oh.

Naoise   It's a candle.

She takes the candle.

Faye   Lovely.

Naoise   A house-warming present, like.

Faye   That's very kind of you.

Naoise   Bergamot.

Faye   Sorry?

Naoise   Bergamot. That scent. It's bergamot.

Faye   Is that a flower?

Naoise   I don't know.

Faye   Right.

Naoise   I didn't realise you still had Mummy's wardrobe.

Faye   Aye, I've had it for years. She didn't have any jewellery so. I had to take something.

Naoise   Do you remember playing 'Detective' in there?

Faye   No.

Naoise   Do you not remember? You set up a detective agency and used the wardrobe as your office.

Faye   Did I?

Naoise   You used to wear Daddy's trench coat.

Faye   And what did we do? Did we solve crimes?

Naoise   Well, you wouldn't let me be a detective. You made me a sort of femme fatale client. To be fair I loved it. It was a very dramatic role.

Beat.

It's really good to see you.

Faye   It's really good to see you too, Naoise. I'm glad you called.

Naoise   I wasn't sure you'd answer.

Faye   I was actually thinking of calling you.

Naoise   Really? Great minds.

Faye *puts the candle down.*

Faye   Aye.

Naoise   Why?

Faye   I need to ask you a favour.

Naoise *is touched by this.*

Naoise   Really?

Faye Just a small favour.

Naoise Absolutely. I mean. Jesus, Faye. Anything.

Faye Brilliant.

Naoise I'd do anything for you.

Faye Great, listen / so

Naoise No, Faye. Sorry. Can I? I'd like to. I owe you an apology.

Faye Oh no, Naoise. Don't worry about it.

Naoise No please let me. I'm sorry I haven't been here for you. I don't think I really knew how to deal with what happened so. I didn't deal with it. Which I realise now, is the worst thing I could have done. Just fucking disappear on you after the break-in. I was going through some shit at the time, I was drinking a lot.

And I can't.

Tell you.

How bad I feel.

Faye Naoise, it's fine.

Naoise You don't have to make me feel better. I just want you to know.
What I'm saying is. I don't want to be like that anymore.
I want to be here for you.
I want to help you.
You're my little sister.
You're my family.
You're my only family.
We have to look after each other.
I'm so relieved you feel like you can ask me for something.
So of course. Of course I'll do you a favour.
Anything.
What do you need me to do?

Faye   I need you to get in the wardrobe.

Beat.

Naoise   Sorry?

Faye   I need you to get in the wardrobe.

Naoise *looks at the wardrobe then at* **Faye**.

Naoise   One more time?

Faye   I need you to get in that wardrobe.

Naoise   Why?

Faye   Basically right, I am fine.

Naoise   Uh-huh.

Faye   You know, I'm over what happened. It wasn't pleasant. But I've been to therapy, I'm in a new flat, and I'm fine.

Naoise   Great. That's great, Faye.

Faye   But recently I've been having a different issue.

Naoise   What's that?

Faye   I can't sleep.

Naoise   Right.

Faye   I haven't slept in about three weeks and I'm sort of going out of my head.

Naoise   You haven't slept in how long?

Faye   Twenty nights. To be exact.

Naoise   No sleep at all?

Faye   Not a wink.

Naoise   Fuck me.

Faye   Thank you.

Naoise   I mean fuck.

Faye   That's exactly the reaction I was hoping for.

Naoise   That's a long time.

Faye   It fucking is a long time.

Naoise   I mean. Jesus. How are you awake right now?

Faye   I don't know.

Naoise   Have you been drinking water?

Faye   Naoise, I'm drowning in it.

Naoise   Have you been exercising?

Faye   I have the arse run off myself.

Naoise   What about the drink?

Faye   I'm not even getting drunk anymore, I polished off a half bottle of whiskey the other night and I just threw it all back up.

Naoise   That's disappointing.

Faye   It was disappointing.

Naoise   Have you been to the doctor?

Faye   Awk, they're no help.

Naoise   What did they say?

Faye   Stupid things. Like, 'You will sleep again, Faye, I know it doesn't feel like it but you will sleep again. Sure, otherwise, you'd die.'

Naoise   What are you supposed to do with that?

Faye   I know. It's so fucking flippant.

Naoise   It is.

Faye   Here actually, is flippant a word?

Naoise   Flippant. It is, aye.

Faye   Doesn't sound like a word.

Naoise   Does it not? Flippant.

Faye   Sounds more like a fruit. Or a cereal. I don't like it.

Naoise   Glib, I think it means.

Faye   Glib?

Naoise   Glib, aye. I think.

Faye   I like that word even less, Naoise.

Naoise   Right, well we'll move away from all of that. Why do you think you're not sleeping?

Faye   I've been thinking about this. I've really been trying to identify what exactly is keeping me awake.

Naoise   Okay.

Faye   When I'm lying in bed at night my hearing gets sharper. Then my heart starts racing and my brain starts whirring. Next thing I'm sweating buckets and I keep thinking I hear someone at my door, at my window, in my flat, and I've figured it out.

Naoise   What is it?

Faye   I'm frightened.

Naoise   Course you are, Faye.

Faye   Even though I'm fine.

Naoise   I know.

Faye   Moment to moment, really, I feel good.

Naoise   Aye.

Faye   It's just because someone broke in once, my brain seems to think it's rational for that to happen again.

Naoise   That makes sense.

Faye   And no matter how many times someone says it's not going to happen, I don't believe them.

Naoise   That's fair.

Faye   Because when I'm lying in bed at night I have this intense feeling that I'm about to be murdered.

Naoise   Murdered?

Faye   Raped and murdered.

Naoise   Oh.

Faye   Aye. So. I talked to some doctors and I've done some research online.

Naoise   On the internet?

Faye   The web, aye. And I've found out about this thing called exposure therapy.

Naoise   Right.

Faye   So you expose yourself to your fear in a safe environment and it helps you to get over it.

Naoise   Mmmm.

Faye   And I think if I could do that, if we could do the exposure therapy together, I'd be able to sleep again. Because I think it's the fear that's keeping me up, Naoise. And I just need to expose myself to it.

Naoise   But your fear is getting raped and murdered.

Faye   That's part of it.

Naoise   How do we expose you to that?

Faye   No, Naoise. Don't be silly.

Naoise   Okay, sorry.

Faye   We don't have to go that far.

Naoise   Good.

Faye   No, I'm scared of someone hiding in the flat waiting to attack me. And I can't erase that memory. So I need to change that memory.

Naoise   Right.

Faye   If I could picture that the man hiding in the flat was just you, I think I would feel better. If the monster in the wardrobe was you, I think I'd feel safe again.

Beat.

Okay. So how do we do that?

Faye   You get in the wardrobe.

Naoise   Okay.

Faye   Then you come out. Take off your mask and / I'll

Naoise   Mask?

Faye   Mask.

Naoise   What mask?

Faye   This mask. He was wearing a mask.

Faye *takes out the duck mask.*

Faye   So you come out. Take the mask off and I'll see it's just you.

Beat.

Naoise   I'm not sure, Faye.

Faye   What?

Naoise   I don't feel comfortable doing that. Not after what happened to you.

Faye   Why?

Naoise   It feels weird.

Faye   I thought you wanted to help me.

Naoise   I do want to help you.

Faye   You said you'd do anything. You literally said anything.

Naoise   I know, I did say that but /

Faye   But not this? Getting into a wardrobe, it's a step too far is it?

Naoise   No, I didn't mean that.

Naoise   Could you not ask someone else to do it?

Faye   I don't have anyone else. And I need it to be you. I feel safe with you.

Beat.

Faye   I haven't asked you for anything in years. I haven't seen you in a year. I know this might not make sense to you, but it makes sense to me.

Naoise   Faye /

Faye   Naoise, I believe people have to take control of their lives. This thing happened to me and I got over it. I won't allow myself to be victim a second time. I can fix this, I can fix anything, I just need your help. Please? I know in my heart this will help me sleep again.

Naoise *looks at the wardrobe again.*

Naoise   Okay.

Faye   Really?

Naoise   Let's do it quick before I change my mind.

Faye   Okay brilliant!

Naoise   What do you need me to do?

Faye   It'll be so easy. You get in the wardrobe and I'm going to play some music. Once you hear it, wait about thirty seconds then get out. Then all you have to do is take off your mask.

Naoise   Then what?

Faye   Then it'll be finished. Would you like a drink before we do it?

Naoise   No thanks.

Faye   Ah, have a drink.

Naoise   Okay.

Faye   Rum?

Naoise   Rum is fine.

Faye   There's rum in this.

She picks up the two-litre bottle of Diet Coke and hands it to him.

Naoise   There's rum in this?

Faye   Rum and Coke. It's as normal as beans on toast.

He takes a delicate sip.

Faye   It's nice isn't it?

She takes a swig.
He takes another delicate sip.

Faye   We can talk too, while you have your drink. Make some conversation, would you like that? To gear ourselves up for the main event.

Naoise   Okay.

Faye   What would you like to talk about?

Naoise   Anything.

Faye   General sort of chit-chat? Aye? Okay. Okay. Topics. Your marriage. What's going on with Hazel?

Naoise   Not that, something else. Let's talk about something else.

He takes a swig.

Faye   Okay. Jobs. How's the university?

Naoise   Fine.

Faye   Do you like your students?

Naoise   Aye.

Faye   Great.

She nods.

Faye   What other topics are there?

Naoise   Why don't we just get this out of the way?

Faye   Absolutely.

Naoise   Yes. Are we just doing it once?

Faye   Let's do it once and then have a chat?

Naoise   So I hop in, wait thirty seconds into the song, hop out, take my mask off and you see it's me.

Faye   That's it. Perfect. Now. Pop on the mask.

Naoise *does.*

Faye   Perfect

He gets in the wardrobe.

Faye *closes the door.*

Three

And He Kindly Assaulted Me

Faye *turns down the lights and takes a long swig of the rum and Diet Coke.*
Faye *takes another swig of the Diet Coke.*
She stands still for a second, thinking.
She removes her knickers and drapes them over a nearby lamp.
She readies herself and then turns on some music – 'Feels Like I'm In Love' by Kelly Marie.

Faye *picks up the mop and starts to dance.*
28 seconds into the song the wardrobe door slowly opens and **Naoise**
gets out, wearing the duck mask.
He watches **Faye**.
He clears his throat but she doesn't hear him.
He closes the wardrobe door loudly.
Still nothing from **Faye**.
The music is too loud for **Faye** *to hear.*
Naoise *feels awkward, so he walks right up to her and touches her
on the shoulder.*
She turns suddenly and hits him on the arm with the mop.
The music is still blaring.

Naoise   Oooooooowww fuck!

Faye *stands ready to fight*

Faye   COME ON /

Naoise   My fucking arm.

Faye   COME / ON

Naoise   That really hurt.

Faye   What?

Naoise   Jesus.

He takes off his mask. He's hurt, physically and emotionally.

Faye   Naoise. Fuck.

Naoise   I can't breathe, Faye. Why did you do that?

Faye   I'm sorry, I'm sorry.

Naoise   You hit me.

Faye   I know.

Naoise   That really hurt.

Faye   It was a reflex.

Naoise   What?

Faye   It was a reflex.

Naoise   Turn that off.

Faye   What?

Naoise   Turn it off.

Faye *turns the music off and turns the lights back on.*
They stand panting.
Naoise *inspects his arm.*

Naoise   Jesus.

Faye   I really wasn't expecting. I wasn't expecting that.

Naoise   You told me to do that.

Faye   No, sorry, I wasn't expecting the feeling I got there.
That was great.

Naoise   Faye, my arm. This is my throwing arm.

Faye   What do you need to throw?

Naoise   Loads of things. Why are you asking that?

Faye   Alright. I'm sorry. Are you alright?

Naoise   No.

Faye   Is anything broken?

Naoise   I'm not an x-ray machine.

Beat.

Faye   Can we do it again?

Naoise   No.

Faye   Please?

Naoise   No I don't want to do it again. You went for me
there.

Faye   I know, but once the music started playing, I got into
it and I realised I could defend myself.

Naoise   You didn't need to defend yourself.

Faye   No I just mean, I hadn't considered the possibility that I could actually defend myself in a situation like this. I could be prepared.

Naoise   What?

Faye   Do you mind if we do it again?

Naoise   Fuck no. This hurts.

Faye   We'll just do it one more time. You overpower me and I'll defend myself.

Naoise   Overpower you?

Faye   You can use this rock.

Naoise   Why do you have a rock in here?

Faye   I like rocks.

Beat.

Naoise   Faye, what are you on about?

Faye   I want to be able to defend myself.

Naoise   Then take a self-defence class.

Faye   No, do you not see that this is perfect? I need to practise in my own home. Let's do it one more time.

Naoise   So you can attack me?

Faye   No, so *you* can attack *me*!

Naoise   Faye, what are you talking about?

Faye   I want to be ready for when it happens again.

Naoise   When what happens again?

Faye   When someone breaks in again.

Naoise   Look Faye I know you think that's rational but it's not.

Faye   Well it happened once. And they never caught the person that broke in the first time. What's to say he won't come back?

Beat.

Faye   Look, that didn't go as planned and I am sorry I hurt you but I can already feel this helping me. Can we do it again?

Naoise   You're asking me to attack you.

Faye   Not a real attack, Naoise. Just pretend. You're just going to pretend to attack me.

Naoise   No.

Faye   We'll choreograph it. Like a dance. It'll be exactly like acting.

Naoise   I'm not an actor.

Faye   No but you did Speech and Drama.

Naoise   When I was nine.

Faye   It won't even take long. It'll be over before you know it. Lickidy split.

Naoise   No, Faye. I'm not going to attack you.

Faye   Why not?

Naoise   It's not going to prepare you even if there is a next time.

Faye   It might not happen exactly the way we practise but it'll help.

Naoise   Faye, I don't want to attack you. I'm not comfortable with it.

Faye   No but you were comfortable not talking to me for a fucking year.

Naoise   I said I was sorry.

Faye   Just now, when I saw you, I felt like I was back there. I could see him step out of the wardrobe. But this time I realised I could defend myself. And it felt great. If we could just do it one more time I could prove to myself that there's a way out. That I'm not trapped. Please?

Beat.

Naoise   Can I ask. I know he hit you but did he touch you?

Faye   I don't know.

Naoise   You don't know?

Faye   I don't think so.

Naoise   What do you remember?

Faye   My head. I felt my head before I opened my eyes, the pain of it. It was thumping. Then I opened my eyes and I saw his penis. And the mask.

Naoise   Do you think he was about to /

Faye   I don't know. He ran out after I opened my eyes.

Beat.

Naoise *gestures to the wardrobe.*

Naoise   Do you actually think this will help?

Faye   One hundred percent.

Naoise   Alright. One more time.

Faye   Really?

Naoise   Aye. No weapons, alright?

Faye   No weapons. Alright. Great. So this time can you try and pin me?

Naoise   What?

Faye   Pin me?

Naoise   To the ground?

Faye   Aye, that's it.

Naoise *resigns.*

Naoise   Right.

Faye   And if you hit me a bit, it's OK.

Naoise   If I hit you a bit?

Faye   That was a joke. Just pin me on the ground. And I'll try to overpower you.

Naoise   Without hurting me?

Faye   I'll go slow. Do you want to hop back in the wardrobe?

Naoise   Fine.

Faye   This time don't take your mask off when you come out. And don't worry about the timing of it. Come out whenever you like.

Naoise   Fine.

Faye   Great. Do you need some ice for your arm or are you alright?

Naoise   Ice would be nice.

Slight pause.

Faye   I don't know why I offered you ice, I don't have any ice. I don't have a freezer. Do you want to pop back in the wardrobe?

Naoise *puts the mask back on.*

Faye   Naoise, thank you.

He gets back in the wardrobe and she closes the door.

Faye *tries to regulate her breathing.*

Faye *takes another swig of the Diet Coke and checks her knickers are still on the lamp.*

She puts on 'Feels Like I'm In Love' by Kelly Marie, from the top.
She starts to dance but almost immediately the wardrobe door flies
open and **Naoise** *comes straight out.*
Faye *turns and gets a genuine fright.*
They stand staring at each other for a moment.
Faye *goes to pull his mask off but he grabs her wrist.*
In an attempt to pull her wrist away from him, **Faye** *falls over.*
Naoise *stands over her and* **Faye** *becomes paralysed with fear.*
He bends down, pinning her wrists.
The music is still blaring.
Faye *starts to struggle underneath him.*
He leans down further and the beak of the duck mask presses into her
face.
He doesn't know what to do next so he just stays there.

Faye   Get off me.

Naoise *doesn't move.*

Faye   Get off me.

Naoise *doesn't move.*

A bright light starts to flash on and off.
Faye *starts to buck.*

Faye   Get off me. Get off me. Get off me. Get off me.

In one movement she shoves him off her.

Faye   Get the fuck off me.

Normal light returns.
Naoise *takes the mask off.*
After a moment, he turns the music off.
Faye *stays curled up in a ball on the floor.*

Naoise   Are you okay? I told you I didn't want to do that. I fucking told you.

Faye *doesn't respond.*

Naoise   I feel sick. Faye? Are you okay?

Faye   Yes.

Naoise   Faye, I didn't want to do that. Are you okay?

Faye   I'm fine.

Naoise   It's not fine. You're not fine.

Faye   I'm fine. (*Beat.*) Let's do it again.

Naoise   What? No, Faye, fuck that. No way.

Faye   I want to do it again, it's helping.

Naoise   It's not helping. It can't be helping. I feel sick.

Faye   It is helping.

Naoise   This is making me sick.

Faye   It's fine.

Naoise   I can't do this.

Faye   It's fine, Naoise, it's helping.

Naoise   I can't do this. I have to tell you something, Faye.

Faye   No, let's go again.

Naoise   Faye, I have to tell you something.

Faye   Tell me later, tell me after.

Naoise   I can't.

Faye   Why?

Naoise   Something's happened.

Faye   Do you have to tell me now?

Naoise   I fucked up, I fucked up.

Faye   What?

Naoise   I've been suspended from work.

Faye   Why?

Naoise   I was suspended last week.

Faye   For what?

Naoise   It's, I. I've.

Faye   For what Naoise?

Naoise   I've been accused of sexual assault. By a woman I work with.

A bright light flashes, illuminating the wardrobe.

Naoise *and* **Faye** *stand looking at each other.*

Refrain Two

Scarlet, Oxblood and Carmine

A bright light flashes, illuminating the wardrobe.
The drum beat returns from the first refrain but it turns into something softer.
Something like 'Yes Sir, I Can Boogie' by Baccara.
Naoise *leaves.*
Faye *stands stock still but alert.*
She starts to scream but nothing comes out, she realises she's lost her voice.
She tries to gather herself but then she starts to sniff the air suspiciously.
Duck Man *comes out of the wardrobe holding a red cape made out of women's knickers.*
Faye *senses his presence and turns around.*
She and **Duck Man** *eye each other for a moment, then he starts spinning the cape in the fashion of a matador, taunting a bull.*
Faye *starts pawing the ground with her feet, as if she was sending dirt flying behind her. She hunches her shoulders, lowers her head and charges at him.*
Duck Man *swiftly moves out of the way.*
Faye *charges again.*
Again **Duck Man** *steps out of the way.*
Faye *charges one last time and misses* **Duck Man** *but gets tangled in the cape.*

The **Duck Man** *slow dances with her.*
He dips her then pulls the cape off her slowly as he gets back in
wardrobe.
Faye *moves back into her starting position.*
Naoise *returns.*

Four

I Find Out What Happened

Music snaps off as lights change.

Faye   Sexual assault?

Naoise   Faye. It's not what it sounds like. It was just a kiss.

Faye   You said sexual assault.

Naoise   I know but it's not really sexual assault.

Faye   It's not really sexual assault?

Naoise   It was a kiss so it's only technically sexual assault.

Faye   Only technically sexual assault?

Naoise   This isn't coming out right.

Faye   Did you or did you not sexually assault someone
Naoise?

Beat.

Naoise   It's not that black and white.

Faye   Wow. Wow. It's not that black and white, fuck off.
Fuck off. (*Beat.*) Why are you telling me this?

Naoise   I'm sorry.

Faye (*looking at the mask*)   You've ruined this, you've fucking
ruined this.

Naoise   I had to tell someone.

Faye   You had to tell someone?

Naoise   Aye.

Faye   And you picked me to tell?

Naoise   Aye.

Faye   Is that why you called me? Is that why you came here, because of this?

Naoise   Not entirely.

Faye   Oh, you fucking scumbag. You didn't want to apologise to me at all.

Naoise   I did, Faye, I did want to apologise, I just didn't know when was the right time.

Faye   Well, you've hit the nail on the head here, mate. Perfect timing. Bang on.

Naoise   Faye, I really didn't want to tell you like this.

Faye   Why did you tell me at all? What made you think I was the right person to tell? In what dimension am I the only person you have to tell about your special sexual assault.

Naoise   I don't trust anyone else.

Faye   What about your wife?

Naoise   I can't tell Hazel.

Faye   Why not?

Naoise   She's pregnant.

Faye   She's what?

Naoise   Hazel's pregnant.

Faye   She's pregnant?

Naoise   Six months.

Faye   Six months.

Naoise   Aye.

Beat.

Faye   I feel sick.

Naoise   Faye.

Faye   I haven't heard sight nor sound of you in twelve months and this, this is what you come to me with.

Naoise   I really did want to apologise.

Faye   Great apology. Could you not have told me after?

Naoise   After what?

Faye   After we finished with the exposure, the therapy.

Naoise   I couldn't keep doing that.

Faye   No, I'm sure it was affecting your gentle nature.

Naoise   I'm sorry Faye.

Faye   I don't see how you could be.

Naoise   It's a woman I work with.

Faye   I don't want to know, Naoise. I don't want to know.

Naoise   If you just let me explain.

Faye   I do not want to know.

Naoise   This woman, Brona, this poor woman. She's a caterer in the university, she works in the canteen.

Faye   Poor? Why poor?

Naoise   I mean, sorry, I meant like, I don't think she's very well.

Faye   In what way?

Naoise   In the head like. She suffers with her nerves or depression or something.
Everyone knows it. She's not well.

Faye   She's not well and you sexually assaulted her?

Naoise   I didn't sexually assault her, we kissed. I thought it was consensual. She's saying it wasn't.

Faye   I don't believe you.

Naoise   Faye, I promise you.

Beat.

Naoise   Please don't look at me like that. Just let me explain, if you just let me explain you'll understand it's a misunderstanding.

Faye   That's a big ask.

Naoise   Please. I'm your brother.

Beat.

Faye   Tell me exactly what happened.

Naoise   Okay.
We used to flirt. I did flirt with her. I put my hands up there. We flirted.
Every lunch, not every lunch but like. At lunch.
She's a nice girl. She used to give me a mountain of chips. Genuinely Faye, too many chips. They'd be spilling off the tray.
I liked her.
I thought she was my friend.
I thought we were friends.
We were out in the pub last week, it was a staff night out and I had asked if she was going. She said she was and she did. But she came on her own, and she was still wearing her catering uniform, it's like a white tunic. It was filthy, there was dried mashed potato and gravy all down it. People were making fun of her. The students.

Some of the lads from work as well. Laughing and that. And Brona's not stupid. She knew they were laughing at her. But she kept trying to sit beside me, the girl was smitten with me, Faye. Her focus was totally on me. So she was sitting at the table with us, not really getting involved in the conversation and one of the lads, Tommy, he's a dick, he rocked the table and Brona's whole pint of Guinness spilled down her top. The whole fucking thing, it went everywhere. She was mortified, she ran off and locked herself in one of the disabled toilets.

Faye   And you went in after her.

Naoise   I did go in after her, aye to see if she was alright. She was crying, Faye, I felt sorry for her. She's like a human puppy. I knocked on the door and she let me in. We had a chat, that's all. I was being nice. But. Then she started to come onto me. She started talking about wanting to fuck me in the industrial fridge in work.

Faye   The industrial fridge?

Naoise   Some fantasy she had.

Then she took her knickers off. Put them in my face.

Faye   She took her knickers off?

Naoise   I thought she kissed me.

Faye   You kissed her back?

Naoise   Aye.

Faye   But you're married.

Naoise   I was drunk. I wasn't thinking straight.

Faye   You're married.

Naoise   I thought it would just be one kiss.

Faye   You're married you, had a fucking wedding. You have a pregnant fucking wife.

Naoise   I know okay, I know. I'm an idiot, but that's all I am.

Faye   Is that all she's accused you of?

Naoise   Yes.

Faye   What did her complaint say?

Naoise   What?

Faye   What did her complaint say?

Naoise   She says I followed her into the bathroom and forced the kiss on her.

Faye   Forced?

Naoise   That's the word she used.

Faye   Forced?

Naoise   Yes.

Faye   You forced yourself on her?

Naoise   I don't think so.

Faye   Why did you follow her?

Naoise   I was trying to be nice, I didn't want her to think I was laughing at her as well.

Faye   You could have spoken to her through the door.

Naoise   I was trying to be nice.

Faye   So has she made this all up then?

Naoise   She has a different perspective.

Faye   Do you think I have a different perspective of what happened to me?

Naoise   No.

Faye   Well I was drunk. Maybe I'm not remembering it correctly. Maybe I was flirting with someone at the party. Maybe I invited them back. Maybe I asked them to hit me over the head and stand over me with their dick out.

Naoise   No I believe you.

Faye   But you don't believe Brona?

Naoise   I think she has a different perspective.

Faye   And why do you think she felt the need to share her different perspective with your employers?

Naoise   Maybe I hurt her. Obviously she's hurt. I've hurt her. For her to say all this.
She must be in an awful state, but her accusation means my job is on the line now.
And I'm positive she kissed me.

Faye   I can't understand why you'd kiss someone you worked with.

Naoise   You're not married.

Faye   I wish I was married to Hazel, she's gorgeous.

Naoise   I love Hazel, but she's not affectionate.

Faye   You were so desperate for affection you forced yourself on a co-worker?

Naoise   I didn't force myself on anyone, I'm not a predator. I flirt with women to make myself feel better. I want them to fancy me. But I never intend to do anything about it. I just want the thrill of a kiss maybe happening, and yes this time it happened but it was a mistake.

Beat.

Do you believe me?

Faye   Does it matter?

Naoise   It does to me.

Naoise   Fuck. Look. Faye. I need to ask you for something.

Faye   Sorry?

Naoise   Like I said, my job is on the line. And. And I need to ask you for something.

Faye   What?

He takes another swig.

Naoise   After what happened to you, awk like you have to understand I would never want . . . What happened to you made me so angry.
Brona's made an official complaint and I've been suspended from work. She hasn't gone to the police. At the moment the university is investigating the complaint. They want to speak to me.

Beat.

I spoke to a solicitor. He can't go in with me because it's an investigation at the moment. He advised me to cooperate, which I am more than willing to do but he suggested I get. Eh. He said I should get a character witness statement. From a woman.

Beat.

Faye *looks at him.*

Faye   You should do that then.

Naoise   That's what I wanted to talk to you about.

Faye   Are you joking?

Naoise   I know this is the worst timing in the world but I didn't do this, Faye. I can't believe I'm doing this to you but I need someone that knows me to write this. I can't ask Hazel. I need you. I need you to tell them you don't think I could ever hurt a woman like that.

Faye *doesn't respond.*

Naoise   I've written it for you.

He talks a piece of paper out of his pocket.

I just need you to sign it.

Faye   No.

Naoise   Please, Faye.

Faye No.

Naoise Faye.

Faye You have balls of steel.

Naoise Faye, I'm fucking desperate here. The meeting is tomorrow morning.

Faye You've left it fairly late.

Naoise I'm on unpaid leave now. Hazel's stopped working already so there's nothing coming in. If I lose this job, I'll not be able to teach ever again. No one hires sex offenders to educate. If I lose the job, I'll lose the house. I've missed one mortgage payment already. I'll lose everything.

Faye Ask one of your friends, ask a woman you work with, ask literally anyone else but me.

Naoise I don't have anyone else.

Faye Why not?

Naoise I don't know. I never really. I never really had female friends, I never really had a lot of friends.

Faye Surely you know some women?

Naoise Aye but /

Faye Aye but what?

Naoise I'm not really friendly with them. Women don't really like me.

Faye Maybe you don't like women.

Naoise Of course I like women.

Faye Do you?

Naoise Yes. I mean. You could always be nicer couldn't you? Everyone could be nicer.

Faye What the fuck does that mean?

Naoise   I'm nice to Hazel.

Faye   If I remember correctly you treated Hazel like shit when we were teenagers.

Naoise   No I didn't.

Faye   I distinctly remember you at a party explaining to the whole room exactly why women aren't funny, directly after Hazel told a joke.

Naoise   I was being ironic, of course some women are funny. Sure there's loads of them, that's just fucking maths.

Faye   You weren't being ironic. You were being cruel. I remember sitting there watching you and thinking: why is he doing this?

Naoise   It was a bad joke, I was locked. I was a teenager. We all say things we regret when we're drunk.

Beat.

I'm sorry, Faye, OK? I'm sorry. I don't want to have this conversation with you. I don't want to do this to you after everything you've been through but I'm scared. Anyone can just say anything about you and your life is fucked. Anyone can come out of the woodwork and say, 'He did a shitty thing to me when he was fifteen and he needs to be punished.' There's no room for growth, how can you learn if you can't make mistakes.

Does an apology mean nothing?

Do I have to keep fucking apologising for every mistake I make?

Faye   Have you ever cheated on Hazel before?

Naoise   What?

Faye   You heard me.

Naoise   No.

Faye   Tell me the truth.

Naoise I haven't.

Faye Have you asked another woman for a drink while you've been married?

Naoise That's a broad question.

Faye Do your best.

Naoise I don't know. Once. Maybe a few times. A handful of times, I don't know what I say every day. What are you doing?

Faye Trying to find out if there's a pattern.

Naoise Pattern of what?

Faye Abuse.

Naoise Well to be fair, Faye, you'd have to trust me to answer those questions truthfully and I don't think you trust me right now.

Faye No, you're right, I don't trust you.

Beat.

Faye I didn't realise you were capable of something like this.

Naoise Capable of what? Asking a girl to after work drinks?

Faye That's not what you were doing.

Beat.

I'm not a bad guy, Faye.

Faye I don't know what you are.

Faye I never even considered you'd be capable of something like this.

Naoise I'm not capable of it.

Faye It stays with you, Naoise. This will stay with that girl.

Naoise   Faye, I swear she kissed me, she put her knickers in my face.

Faye   You can't prove that.

Naoise   There's a lot of things that you can't prove but I still believe you.

Beat.

Faye   You know, I don't think there's anything wrong with my brain. I think I'm right to be scared of being attacked.

Naoise   I'd never do anything to you.

Beat.

Faye   That's not what I meant.

Beat.

Naoise   Jesus I know. I didn't mean that. Just. Fuck. Have you never hurt anyone Faye?

Faye   What?

Naoise   Have you ever hurt anyone?

Faye   Of course I have.

Naoise   You seem to be so perfect.

Faye   I seem to be so perfect, because I'm appalled at you?

Naoise   Did you ever kiss anyone you shouldn't have?

Faye   We're not talking about me.

Naoise   I'm talking about you. Did you ever force yourself on anyone?

Faye   No.

Naoise   Are you sure?

Faye   I'm fucking positive.

Naoise   How positive?

Faye What are you getting at, Naoise?

Beat.

Naoise You don't remember forcing yourself on me?

Faye *doesn't respond for ages.*

Faye What?

Naoise When we were kids. You forced yourself on me?

Faye I can't believe you.

Naoise You don't remember? When we were playing 'Detective'. You kissed me.

Faye No I didn't.

Naoise Are you calling me a liar?

Faye I am your sister, how would I force myself on you.

Naoise We were playing and you grabbed me by the shoulders and kissed me on the mouth.

Faye I have literally no recollection of that. And if it did happen, I was a child. I didn't know what I was doing.

Naoise It did happen. You crossed a line.

Faye With a kiss?

Naoise Aye.

Faye It was just a kiss, Naoise.

Naoise Exactly.

Faye What are you trying to do? Is this your defence? I was a child. How could I be accountable for that? You're an adult.

Naoise Well let's talk about some things you did when you were an adult. Sure time you were out, you were taking your clothes off at a house party.

This stops **Faye**.

Faye   Sorry?

Naoise   That house party. A year ago, you did a striptease on the kitchen table. You took your knickers off.

Faye   How did you know about that?

Naoise   What?

Faye   How did you know about that? Did someone tell you?

Naoise   No.

Faye   That was the night I was attacked. How did you know, Naoise?

Faye *realises both the rock and the mop are now behind* **Naoise**.

Beat.

Naoise   Faye, are you joking?

Faye   No.

Naoise   I was there.

Faye   Where?

Naoise   At the party.

Faye   I didn't know you were at the party.

Naoise   Yes you did.

Faye   No I didn't.

Naoise   I was talking to you.

Faye   What?

Naoise   I walked you home.

Faye   No you didn't.

Naoise   Oh my God. What is this, Faye? Are you saying you don't remember?

Faye   I don't remember you being there.

Naoise It's why I stopped talking to you. I was angry at you for embarrassing me at the party. Taking all your fucking clothes off. Then when I heard what happened to you I felt guilty. I felt so guilty because I should have walked you into the house. If I'd have just come into the house I would have seen him.

Beat.

Faye? Faye?

She moves back from **Naoise**.

Faye I'll sign the letter.

Naoise What?

Faye I'll sign it.

Naoise Really?

Faye I'll sign it now if you just do one thing for me?

Naoise Okay.

Faye Can you get back in the wardrobe one last time?

Six

And I Asked to See His Penis

Faye *and* **Naoise** *stand still.*

Naoise I don't think so, Faye.

Faye I'm not asking you to do anything, I'm not asking you to come out and attack me. I just want to end the night with a visual of you in there.

Naoise I don't want to.

Faye It's the only way I can see myself having a chance at sleep.

Naoise *doesn't respond.*

Faye   Please?

Naoise   Will you sign it?

Faye   Yes.

Naoise   Do you promise?

Faye   I swear.

Naoise   Swear to me, Faye.

Faye   Naoise, I swear. I'll sign it the second you come out.

Beat.

Naoise   I'm not putting the mask on.

Faye   Fine.

Naoise   And I don't want the music on.

Faye   No problem.

Naoise   How long do you want me to stay in?

Faye   Just ten seconds. Then you can come out.

Naoise *walks over to the wardrobe.* **Faye** *follows behind him.*

Naoise   Ten seconds?

Faye   Ten.

He gets in and she closes the door.

Naoise   Ten.
Nine.
Eight.

Faye *walks over and picks up the rock.*

Naoise   Seven.
Six.
Five.
Four.

Faye *stands in the corner of the room, furthest away from the wardrobe.*

Naoise   Three.
Two.
One.

Faye *holds the rock out, as a weapon, and braces herself for* **Naoise** *stepping out of the wardrobe.*

Naoise *opens the door and stops when he sees her.*

Naoise   What are you doing?

Faye   You didn't walk me home that night.

Naoise   What?

Faye   I remember walking home on my own. You didn't walk me home.

Naoise *is silent for a second.*

He goes to move towards her.

Faye   Stay away from me.

Naoise   Faye, what are you talking about?

Faye   You didn't walk me home, Naoise.

Naoise   I did.

Faye   No you didn't. I remember.

Naoise   What are you saying?

Faye   It was you.

Naoise   What?

Faye   I think it was you. I think you got in before me. Christ, you had keys. I think you waited for me. Maybe you just wanted to scare me, but something else took over.

Naoise   You think I attacked you?

Faye   I do.

Naoise   You actually think I attacked you?

Faye   I do.

Naoise   I didn't, Faye.

Faye   Then prove it.

Naoise   How?

Faye   Show me your dick.

Long beat.

Naoise   What?

Faye   Show me your dick.

Naoise   I'm not going to do that, Faye.

Faye   If you don't show it to me, I'll tell Hazel what you did. To her and to me.

Naoise   Please don't talk to Hazel.

Faye   Then show it to me.

Naoise   What the fuck is going on, what's all this?

Faye   If it's not you then you shouldn't have a problem showing me. It's nothing I haven't seen before. Sure we used to take baths together.

Naoise   We were babies then. It was a baby's penis. It's very different now.

Faye   Just take it out.

Naoise   I didn't attack you, Faye. I would never do that.

Faye   Prove it.

Neither of them move.

Faye   Take off your trousers.

Naoise   Faye, I think you're having an episode.

Faye   Don't fucking patronise me.

Naoise   I understand what I just told you is a head fuck but if you just / listen

Faye   Naoise I'll start counting and when I reach one, I'm leaving to speak to your wife.

Naoise   You're acting insane.

Faye   Five.

Naoise   You're starting at five?

Faye   Four.

Naoise   Hang on a second.

Faye   Three.

Naoise   Stop.

Faye   Two.

Naoise   Faye. You really don't want to do this.

Faye   I just want to see your penis, Naoise, is that too much to ask?

Naoise   Can you hear yourself? How could you think I'd do that to you? I'm your brother.

Faye   I don't know who you are.

Naoise   Faye.

Faye   I know it was you, Naoise. I know in my gut you did it. I can feel it now.

Naoise   Faye, it wasn't me

Faye   I don't believe you.

Naoise   I swear.

Faye   I don't believe you.

Naoise   Faye / stop

Faye   Naoise it was you. It's your fault. It's your fault I can't sleep, it's your fault I can't go outside, it's your fault I can't let anyone touch me, it's your fault I can't be normal.

Beat.

Faye   So take it out.

Naoise *removes his trousers and stands there in his boxers.*

Faye   Take it out now.

Naoise   I'm sorry, Faye.

Naoise *puts his hand inside his boxers.*
Naoise *slowly takes his penis out of his boxers.*

Faye *looks at it, then moves closer to inspect it. She gets down on her knees and starts to handle it.*
She looks up at him.
She stands up.
She moves far away from him.

Faye   It's not you.

Naoise *is frozen in shock.*

Faye   It wasn't you.

Refrain Three

Cereal Release

A bright light flashes, illuminating the wardrobe.

Les Fleurs by Minnie Ripperton plays as **Naoise** *is still frozen.*

Faye *turns to the wardrobe and pulls the duck mask out. She puts it on slowly and starts to dance.*

She guides **Naoise** *down to his knees and picks up the box of Rice Krispies.*

She slowly lifts the box over her head then tips the entire box over **Naoise**.

Faye *dances into a spotlight and removes the duck mask as* **Naoise** *wakes from his frozen state and leaves.*

Seven

Cash or Card

A doctor's surgery, somewhere in Ireland.

Dr Hollowman   Faye, lovely to see you again.

Faye   Lovely to see you too, doctor.

Dr Hollowman   I'm delighted to see you doing so well.

Faye   Thank you, doctor. I don't want to talk my luck away but I feel fantastic.

Dr Hollowman   And you've never looked better. How's it going with the girlfriend?

Faye   Wonderful. We've decided to move in together.

Dr Hollowman   Great news. Couples therapy went well then?

Faye   We didn't need it in the end. We just went to one session and the therapist told us she'd never seen a couple so happy or well adjusted in her life. She said we were the last people in the world she should treat.

Dr Hollowman   What a bizarre and wonderful turn-up for the books.

Faye   I know. I thought so too. Speaking of which, did I tell you I got a book deal?

Dr Hollowman   Your memoir?

Faye   Exactly.

Dr Hollowman   Exhilarating.

Faye   And we've been able to buy a house with the advance. A detached house, in the middle of the city. There's a wee stream running through the back garden. It is idyllic.

Dr Hollowman   No one deserves it more. And how's your brother?

Faye   He's great, turns out he was completely innocent.

Dr Hollowman   Wonderful news.

Faye   He didn't need the letter after all.

Dr Hollowman   You truly are my favourite patient, Faye. You've managed to totally turn your situation around. When you came in here you were a mess. You couldn't stop crying, you thought you were going to be murdered all the time.

Faye   I was so wacky.

Dr Hollowman   And now look at you. Successful, beautiful, loved and about to be very wealthy.

Faye   Extremely wealthy.

Dr Hollowman   How did you do it?

Faye   You know, I don't know.
Ever since I was a child, I felt like I took in too much information.
I listened too closely for intonation in people's voices.
I was totally preoccupied by their micro-expressions.
I made up whole stories based on imagined reactions.
It overwhelmed me completely.

Beat.

I tried everything to turn the volume down in my head.
I tried drink and love and sex and cigarettes and focus.
Serious fucking focus.
And I found I could create a sort of violent silence in myself.
I could turn down the noise, the
Why did you say that?
Why did you do that?

Why are you like that?
I could turn it all down.
Because that gets boring after a while.
That perpetual awareness of everyone and everything's very
existence is really fucking dull.
So I just turned it down.
And it was good.
For so long it was good.
Then when I came home to find that man in my house.
He took that silence away from me.

Afterwards I started having nightmares.
Then I stopped being able to go to sleep.
Then I couldn't sleep at all.
I'd get into bed every night and I'd just lie there.
Time would move around me and through me and I'd lie
there and the buzzing in my head became unbearable.
So I got up.
I tried to do things.
I tried to be productive.
I tried to
Read
Write
Squat
Thrift
Recycle
Upcycle
Play piano
Learn Spanish
Do push-ups
Make honeycomb
Make Pavlova
Fight the status quo
Figure out the crash of two thousand and eight
Predict the crash of twenty twenty-eight
Unearth political cronyism in Ireland
Watch the films of Bette Davis
Grow rosemary

Sun dry tomatoes
Adopt a dog
Save for a mortgage
Start sea swimming
Start running
Start a coven
Shop local
Discover Tarot
Take down Amazon
Take up knitting
Take up crochet
Take up embroidery
Buy a loom
Help the poor
Help the sick
Get a silk suit
Do my will
Buy a plot
Philately
You know I wanted to use this extra time to better myself.
This extra time that insomnia was affording me.
This luxury that I had.
But I couldn't.
Words slipped and slid off the page
Bette Davis was a blur
And I didn't even know where I'd put a loom.
There was no room.
In my flat or my head and that when the tears came.
I'd cry and cry all night and that started to bleed into the
day, it was my reaction to everything.
And then people were saying to me;
You're really going to have to get over whatever this is.
And I'd tell them I'm sorry but I'm fine.
I'm having a bad day, I'm on my period, it's hayfever.
I'm sorry I'm sorry I'm sorry
I'm fine.
I wanted it to be true.
But I knew.

It wasn't true.
I knew.
I'm not fine.
I'm not okay.

Beat.

But then I thought about what people had said to me.
You're really going to have to get over whatever this is.
And I thought fuck it.
I should get over it.
So that's what I did.
I cleaned my face, I made some avocado toast, I got a book deal,
And I got over it.
I know you said there's no smash cut to happy doctor, but I really feel like there is.

*A bright light flashes, illuminating the wardrobe and **Faye**'s attention is drawn to it.*

A throbbing light comes from inside the wardrobe.

*The door opens with a bang and **Duck Man** steps out.*

A drum beat starts and something seriously swingy comes on.

like 'Sing, Sing, Sing' by Benny Goodman.

Faye *and* **Duck Man** *break into the swing dance from the first refrain.*

They move in perfect synchronicity this time.

Duck Man *pulls* **Faye** *in, squeezes her, then dips her.*

Faye *puts* **Duck Man** *back in the wardrobe and she spins herself into the spotlight.*

Music snaps off.

The End.